This series prepared in
consultation with the
British Veterinary Association
Animal Welfare Foundation

© Rod Campbell 1990
First published 1990 by
Campbell Books
96 Leonard St · London EC2A 4RH
in association with The Watts Group
All rights reserved
ISBN 1 85292 050 5
Printed in Singapore
10 9 8 7 6 5 4 3 2 1

We have a
Rabbit

Rod Campbell

CAMPBELL BOOKS

We have a rabbit.
I love it very much and
like helping to look
after it . . .

My rabbit needs two meals a day.
I help to feed it grains, fresh greens like cabbage, and water.
It also needs fresh hay.

My rabbit lives outside
in a hutch.
The hutch has a warm dry
sleeping part with hay
and straw.
It also has a living area.

My rabbit needs exercise.
We have a special pen
for it to run around in.

I like to stroke my rabbit.
I lift it up very gently
and hold it carefully
like this . . .

I help to clean my rabbit's hutch every day, and wash it out once a week.
I put fresh straw in its sleeping area.

To keep my rabbit well,
we always visit the Vet.
The Vet is the animals'
doctor.

My rabbit has gone to bed.

Can you see it in the hutch?
Shh...don't wake it up!